TABULATED
BIOGRAPHICAL
HISTORY OF MUSIC

Compiled by

O S C A R   T H O M P S O N

HARCOURT, BRACE AND COMPANY
NEW YORK

Foreword

Everyone interested in the history of music—which is primarily a chronicle of the careers and works of important composers—has felt the need for a volume which could supply the salient facts regarding any great composer or any particular period in condensed tabulated form, obviating the necessity for time-consuming and frequently laborious research in voluminous encyclopedic works.

This volume is designed to serve exactly such a need. If its columns are read downward, the reader secures biographical outlines containing the important events and works of great composers. If read across, the simultaneous events and music works of a given year are found tabulated side by side, providing a record for quick reference of contemporaneous fact and achievement.

It is possible to see, for instance, what Brahms was doing in a particular year of achievement by Wagner; to take in the concurrent activities of Schumann, Chopin, Berlioz and Mendelssohn; to see how Mozart's career was but a segment of that of Haydn's. A glance at the year 1813—as a single instance of the use of the chart—will show the birth of Wagner, the birth of Verdi, the composition of Schubert's first symphony, the advent of Beethoven's seventh symphony and the production of two Rossini operas.

The facts and dates included have been secured from the most reliable standard music reference works. Wherever there has been some doubt or disagreement on dates, the ones generally favored have been adopted. It has not been found feasible to unify in all instances the choice of dates, as between those which are dates of composition, dates of first performance and dates of publication. In a large majority of instances the dates given are those of composition. For many operas, however, the dates are those of first performances.

Oscar Thompson

Biographical Index

For instant condensed information regarding the activities or works of any composer mentioned in this volume, consult the plate and column indicated opposite his name, and read vertically.

Period Index

For instant condensed information regarding musical progress during any special period of time, consult the plate which covers the period in question, and read horizontally.

Plate 1
A.D. 995-1539

PLATE 1- A.D. 995-1539

1	2	3	4	5	6
D'AREZZO (Guido)	DUNSTABLE (John)	BINCHOIS (Gilles)	OKEGHEM (Jean)	DES PRÉS (Josquin)	WILLAERT (Adrian)

Born about A.D.995
Arezzo, Italy

Became a monk in a Benedictine monastery at Pomposa

Traveled in France and England

Visited the Abbey of St. Maur des Fosses

Invented system of Solmisation still in use

Worked with Odo, another monk

Returned to Arezzo; wrote a work called "Micrologus", an epitome of musical knowledge

Called to teach his theories at Papal Court

Made improvements in music staff

Taught intervals by a sliding graduated scale on the ancient monochord

Became Prior of the Camaldolite Fraternity at Avellano, Italy

Died about 1050 (Avellano)

Born Bedfordshire, England about 1370

Nothing known of his life

Mentioned in musical works by Tinctoris and Le Franc

Six volumes of his works discovered at Trent Cathedral in 1884

Works reveal highly developed musical art in England in the early part of 15th Century, antedating the early Italian School

Died 1453 (Walbrook.)

Born in Binche, Belgium about 1400

1425 Became a priest

1437 Chaplain at church in Mons

Composed chansons, sacred songs and masses

Died 1460 (Lille)

Born about 1430 Flanders

1443 Chorister Antwerp Cathedral

1450 Pupil of Dufay

1465 Chapel master at Paris

Wrote 17 masses, 7 motets, 19 secular songs

Died 1495 (Tours)

Born about 1445 Hainault, Burgundy

Studied under Okeghem

1471-1484 Singer in Sistine Chapel, Rome

Wrote a Mass and a Miserere at Ferrara

1490 At Court of Louis XII in Paris

Wrote masses, motets and secular songs

Died 1521 (Condé)

Born about 1480 Bruges, The Netherlands

Studied with Josquin des Prés

1518 Went to Rome

1527 Founded music school at San Marc Venice

PLATE 1-A.D. 995-1539

7	8	9	10	11	12
MORALES (Cristobal)	TALLYS (Thomas)	ARCADELT (Jacob)	PALESTRINA (Giovanni)	LASSUS (Orlando)	BYRD (William)
n about 1500 ille, Spain					
	Born 1510 in England (Place un- known)				
4 Studied at ille Cathedral	Chorister at St. Paul's Cathe- dral	Born about 1514 The Netherlands			
luenced by works Josquin des Prés					
	King's organist at Waltham Abbey				
			Born 1525 in town of Palestrina. near Rome, Italy		
6 Chapel master Avila			Family name was Pierluigi		
				Born 1530 Mons, The Netherlands	
5 in Rome					
8 Wrote cantata Peace Confer- e at Nice				1538-41 In Italy	Born 1538 London, England Pupil of Tallys
		1539 Five books of masses 1539-49 In Papal Choir at Rome	1539 Pupil of Firmin Le Bel		

ontd. Pl. 2, Col. 2) (Contd. Pl. 2, Col. 3) (Contd. Pl. 2, Col. 4) (Contd. Pl. 2, Col. 5) (Contd. Pl. 2, Col. 6) (Contd. Pl. 2, Col. 7)

Plate 2
A. D. 1540-1599

PLATE 2—1540—1599

1	2	3	4	5	6
WILLAERT (Contd.)	MORALES (Contd.)	TALLYS (Contd.)	ARCADELT (Contd.)	PALESTRINA (Contd.)	LASSUS (Contd.)
Founder of Venetian school	1540 Returned to Spain				
Wrote masses, motets, madrigals and songs			1542 Madrigals and French chansons		
	Wrote masses and motets			1544 Organist at Palestrina Cathedral	
Pupils included Zarlino and Cyprian de Rore	Died 1553 (Malaga)				
				1551 Teacher of native singers at St. Peter's, Rome 1555 Admitted to Pontifical Chapel	1554-57 In Antwe
Invented double choruses in church services	VITTORIA (Tommaso) Born 1540 Avila, Spain	Gentleman of the Chapel Royal during the reigns of Henry VIII, Edward VI, Queen Mary and Queen Elizabeth	1555 At Paris in the service of Cardinal Charles of Lorraine		1557-94 In Munic
			1557 Published three masses	1560 "Improperia" for Holy Week use	
Died 1562 (Venice)					
		Composed motets, anthems and church services		1567 Mass for Pope Marcellus	
				1571 Maestro at St. Peter's	
	1573 Maestro Collegium Germanicum				1573-76 Issued Patrocinium
		1575 Granted monopoly on music publishing (with William Byrd) by Queen Elizabeth	Died 1575 (Paris)	Composed 180 motets, 113 hymns, 93 masses, 140 sacred and secular madrigals	Composed about 25 masses, motets, mad gals and secular son
	1585 Motetta Festorum 1589-1602 Royal Chapel at Madrid	Died 1585 (Greenwich)		Died 1594 (Rome)	Died 1594 (Munic

(Contd. Pl. 3, Col. 6)

PLATE 2 – 1540 – 1599

7	8	9	10	11	12
BYRD (Contd.)	GESUALDO (Carlo)	PERI (Jacopo)	MONTEVERDE (Claudio)	GIBBONS (Orlando)	SCHÜTZ (Heinrich)
4 Senior chor- er St. Paul's					
	Born 1560, Naples, Italy				
		Born 1561 Florence, Italy			
3 Organist at coln Cathedral					
			Born 1567 Cremona, Italy		
9 Gentleman of pel Royal					
5 Granted (with mas Tallys) ex- sive music-- nting franchise	1575 Pupil of Pomponio Nenna				
		1583 Maestro to Ferdinand I		Born 1583 Cambridge, England	
			1584-99 Wrote can- zonettas and madrigals		
tributed to en Elizabeth ginal Book		1585 Attached to Grand Ducal Court at Florence			Born 1585 Köstritz, Germany
	1594 First and second books of madrigals 1595-1611 Other madrigal books				
				1596 Chorister at Kings College	
		1597 "Dafne"			
					1599 Chorister at Marburg

td. Pl. 3, Col. 8)(Contd. Pl. 3, Col. 7)(Contd. Pl. 3, Col. 1)(Contd. Pl. 3, Col. 2)(Contd. Pl. 3, Col. 3)(Contd. Pl. 3, Col. 5)

Plate 3
A. D. 1600-1699

PLATE 3—1600—1699

1	2	3	4	5	6
PERI (Contd.)	MONTEVERDE (Contd.)	GIBBONS (Contd.)	CARISSIMI (Giacomo)	SCHÜTZ (Contd.)	VITTORIA (Contd.)
1600 "Euridice"	1602 Maestro to Duke of Mantua				Requiem for Empr Maria
	1603 "Orfeo"	1604 Organist at Chapel Royal Composed sacred works, and pieces for viols	Born 1604 Marino, Italy		
1608 Wrote recitatives for Monte-Verde's opera "Arianna"	1608 "Arianna"			1609 In Venice 1611 Book of madrigals	
1615 "La Guerra d'amore"		1622 Organist at Westminster Abbey		1614 Maestro at Dresden 1619 Psalms of David 1623 "Resurrection" Oratorio	Died 1613 (Madri
		Died 1623 (London)			
	1624 "Tancredi and Clorinda"		1624 Organist Tivoli Cathedral	1627 Opera "Dafne"	
			1628-74 Maestro San Apollinare		
		LULLY (Jean-Baptiste) Born 1632 Florence, Italy			
Died 1633 (Florence)					
BUXTEHUDE (Dietrich) Born 1637 Helsingborg, Sweden	1642 "Coronation of Poppaea" Died 1643 (Venice)				
		1645 Kitchen boy and violinist at French Court 1653 Court composer			CORELLI (Arcangelo) Born 1653 Fusignan Italy
	SCARLATTI (Alessandro) Born 1659 Sicily		1664 Oratorio "Jephtha"		
				1665 Passion and Christmas Oratorio	
1668-1707 Organist Marienkirche (Lübeck) 1673 Established "Abendmusiken", a new form of musical service held on Sunday afternoons		1672 Opened Royal Academy 1673 "Alceste"		Died 1672 (Dresden)	1689-90 At Court Modena
			Died 1674 (Rome)		
		1677 "Isis"		VIVALDI (Antonio) Born 1673 Venice, Italy	
		1680 "Proserpine" 1681 "Le Triomphe de l'Amour"	TELEMANN (Georg) Born 1681 Magdeburg, Germany		
	1682 Went to Naples	1682 "Perseus"			
	1685 Famous son, Domenico, born (See Column 10)	Died 1687 (Paris)			
	1690 Opera "La Rosaura"				
					1694 Trio sonatas da Camera

(Contd. Pl. 4, Col. 8) (Contd. Pl. 4, Col. 5)   (Contd. Pl. 4, Col. 7) (Contd. Pl. 4, Col. 3) (Contd. Pl. 4, Col

PLATE 3—1600—1699

7	8	9	10	11	12
GESUALDO (Contd.)	BYRD (Contd.)	RAMEAU (Jean-Philippe)	SCARLATTI (Domenico)	HANDEL (George Frederick)	BACH (Johann Sebastian)
	Composed church services, masses, madrigals and pieces for virginals and organ				
:d 1613 (Naples)					
	Died 1623 (London)				
PURCELL (Henry) n 1658 London, land					
	COUPERIN (François) Born 1668 Paris				
:0 Organist at tminster					
:2 Organist at apel Royal		Born 1683 Dijon, France			
	1685 Organist at St. Gervais		Born 1685 Naples, Italy	Born 1685 Halle, Germany	Born 1685 Eisenach, Germany
:8 "Dido and eas"					
	1693 Court organist				
:d 1695 (London)					

(Contd. Pl. 4, Col. 2) (Contd. Pl. 4, Col. 1) (Contd. Pl. 4, Col. 6) (Contd. Pl. 4, Col. 10) (Contd. Pl. 4, Col. 11)

Plate 4
A. D. 1700-1724

PLATE 4—1700—1724

1 RAMEAU (Contd.)	2 COUPERIN (Contd.)	3 VIVALDI (Contd.)	4 CORELLI (Contd.)	5 SCARLATTI, A. (Contd.)	6 SCARLATTI, D. (Contd.)
			Composed 12 sonatas for violin and harpsichord	1702 Went to Florence	
	1703-05 Versets de Motets				
				1704 Assistant Chapelmaster at Ste. Maria Maggiore in Rome	
					1705 Visited Florence and Veni
1706 Published first harpsichord pieces				1706 Member of Arcadian Academy with Corelli	
			1708 Visited Naples		
Succeeded father as organist at Cathedral in Avignon					1709 Contest wit Handel in Rome f harpsichord and organ playing.
			1712 Concerti Grossi (Rome)		
	1713 Four books of harpsichord pieces	1713 Director of the Conservatory della Pietà	Died 1713 Rome	1713 Returned to Naples	
1714 Organist at Lyons			GLUCK (Christoph Willibald) Born 1714 Neumarkt, Germany	1715 "Tigrane"	1715 Maestro at St. Peter's, Rom
		Composed 28 operas between 1713 and 1739			
	Appointed harpsichord player to King Louis XV			1718 "Telemaco"	
					1719 Opera harpsichordist in London
					1720 "Narciso"
1722 Published "Trait de L'harmonie"	Director of Royal Concerts at Court			1721 "Griselda" (114th and last opera)	1721 At Lisbon
1723 Settled in Paris					

(Contd. Pl. 5, Col. 8)(Contd. Pl. 5, Col. 21(Contd. Pl. 5, Col. 3)(Contd. Pl. 5, Col. 11)(Contd. Pl. 5, Col. 4)(Contd. Pl. 5, Co

PLATE 4—1700—1724

7	8	9	10	11	12
TELEMANN (Contd.),	BUXTEHUDE (Contd.)	DR. ARNE (Thomas, A.)	HANDEL (Contd.)	BACH, J.S. (Contd.)	PERGOLESI (Giovanni Battista)
0 at Leipzig versity					
			1703 In Hamburg	1703 Violinist in Weimar Orchestra	
4-08 Organist concertmaster Sorau	Regarded as one of the greatest composers of the organ fugue and suite		1704 Composed a "Passion"	1704 Organist at Arnstadt	
			1705 First operas "Almira" and "Nero" (Hamburg)	1705 Walked to Lubeck to hear Buxtehude	
			1706-08 In Italy "Rodrigo" "Agrippina"		
	Died 1707 (Lubeck)			1707 Organist at Muhlhausen Married cousin, Maria Barbara	
9 Conductor Eisenach			1709 In Germany Concertmaster at Hanover	1708 Organist at Weimar	
		Born 1710 London, England	1710 In England "Rinaldo"	1710 Wilhelm Friedemann (oldest son) born Known as the "Halle Bach"	Born 1710 Jesi, Italy
I In Frankfort			1711 In Hanover		
			1712 Returned to England "Il Pastor Fido" "Teseo" Utrecht Te Deum		
			1714 "Water Music"	1714-Third son, Karl Philipp Emanuel, born; known as the "Berlin or Hamburg Bach"	
6 Composed a ssion" to verses Brockes of burg			1716-17 In Hanover Composed "Passion"		
			1718 In England	1717 Concertmaster at Cothen Challenge to Marchand in Dresden	
			1720 Oratorio, "Esther" Opera "Radamisto" "Harmonious Blacksmith"	1719 At Halle, too late to meet Handel 1720 In Carlsbad Death of first wife, Maria Barbara	
1-67 Music ector at burg			1721 "Floridante"	1721 Married Anna Magdalena Wulken	1721 Studied the violin with local teachers
			1723 "Julius Caesar "Ottone" "Flavio"	1722 Book I, "Well-Tempered Clavichord" 1723 Cantor of Thomaschule, Leipzig	
			1724 "Tamerlano"	1724 St. John Passion	

td. Pl. 5, Col. 7)   (Contd. Pl. 5, Col. 6)(Contd. Pl. 5, Col. 9)(Contd. Pl. 5, Col. 10)(Contd. Pl. 5, Col. 1)

Plate 5
A. D. 1725-1749

PLATE 5—1725—1749

1	2	3	4	5	6
PERGOLESI (Contd.)	COUPERIN (Contd.)	VIVALDI (Contd.)	SCARLATTI, A. (Contd.)	SCARLATTI, D. (Contd.)	DR. ARNE (Contd.)
	1725 Concert In-strumental		Died 1725 (Naples)	1725-29 In Naples as harpsichord virtuoso	1725 Violin less with Michael Festing
	1726 Four trio suites				
	1728 Pieces de Viole		PICCINI (Nicola) Born 1728 Bari, Italy		
				1729-54 In Madrid as music-master to the Princess of the Asturias	
					1731 Taught sist Susanna Maria to sing
1733 "La Serva Pa-drona"	Died 1733 Paris				1733 "Rosamond" "Dido and Aenea
	The first great com-poser of harpsichord music in France				
1735 "L'Olympiade"					
1736 "Stabat Mater" Died 1736 (Pozz-uoli, Italy)		1736 Twelve String Trios			
					1738 Incidental m sic to Milton's "Comus"
				1740 Visited Dublin and London	1740 Masque "Alfre containing the famo song "Rule Britann
	GRÉTRY (André) Born 1741 Liege, Belgium				
BOCCHERINI (Luigi) Born 1743 Lucca, Italy		Died 1743 Venice	1742 Studied with Durante for 12 years at Naples		
					1745 "The Temple of Dullness"
					1746 Music for Shakespeare's " Tempest"
		CIMAROSA (Domenico) Born 1749 Aversa, Italy			

(Contd. Pl. 6, Col. 12) (Contd. Pl. 6, Col. 8) (Contd. Pl. 6, Col. 9) (Contd. Pl. 6, Col. 6) (Contd. Pl. 6, Col. 10) (Contd. Pl. 6, Col

PLATE 5-1725-1749

7 TELEMANN (Contd.)	8 RAMEAU (Contd.)	9 HANDEL (Contd.)	10 BACH, J.S. (Contd.)	11 GLUCK (Contd.)	12 HAYDN (Franz Josef)
	1726 Published "New System of Musical Theory"	1726 "Scipione" "Alessandro"			
		1727 "Admeto" "Riccardo Primo"			
		1728 "Siroe" "Tolemeo"			
		1729 Visited Germany	1729 Passion of St. Matthew		
0 "Tod Jesu"		1730 "Partenope"			
		1731 "Poro" "Ezio"			
		1732 "Acis and Galatea"	1732 Johann Christoph born at Leipzig; known as the "Bückeburg Bach"	1732 Learned to play the violin, harpsichord and organ at Jesuit College in Komotau	Born 1732 Rohrau, Austria
	1733 "Hyppolyte et Aricie	1733 Oratorios "Deborah" and "Athalia"			
		1734 "Terpsichore"	1734 Christmas Oratorio		
	1735 "Les Indes galantes"	1735 "Ariodante" "Alcina"	1735 Johann Christian born at Leipzig; known as the "English or London Bach"		
		1736 "Atalanta" "Alexander's Feast"		1736 In Vienna and Milan	
7 In Paris	1737 "Castor et Pollux"	1737 "Arminio" "Giustino" "Berenice" "Trionfo" (Revised)			1737 Evidences of musical ability at age of five
		1738 "Serse" "Faramondo"	1738 B Minor Mass		
	1739 "Dardanus"	1739 Oratorios "Saul" and "Israel in Egypt"			
		1740 "Imeneo"			1740 Went to Vienna as choir boy at Stephen's Church
		1741 "Deidamia" 1742 Oratorio "The Messiah" 1743 "Samson" "Semele" "Joseph" Dettinger Te Deum 1745 "Belshazzar" "Heracles" 1746 "Occasional Oratorio" 1747 "Judas Maccabaeus"		1741 "Artaserse"	
			1744 Part II of "Well-Tempered Clavichord"	1744 "Impermnestra" Poro"	
			1747 Played for King Frederick in Berlin	1746 "La Caduta dei Giganti"	
	1748 "Pygmalion"	1748 "Joshua" 1749 "Solomon" Fireworks Music	1749 "Art of Fugue" Eye Operation Died 1750 (Leipzig)		1748 Dismissed for playing a practical joke

ntd. Pl. 6, Col. 1)(Contd. Pl. 6, Col. 2†(Contd. Pl. 6, Col. 3)   (Contd. Pl. 6, Col. 5)(Contd. Pl. 6, Col. 7)

Plate 6
A. D. 1750-1774

PLATE 6 — 1750 - 1774

1	2	3	4	5	6
TELEMANN (Contd.)	RAMEAU (Contd.)	HANDEL (Contd.)	BACH (Johann Christian) (Born 1735)	GLUCK (Contd.)	PICCINI (Contd.)
		1750 "Theodora"		1750 "Telemaco"	
		1751 "Choice of Hercules"		1751 "Ezio"	
	1752 Controversy of "La Guerre des Bouffons"	1752 "Jephtha" Beginning of blindness		1752 "La Clemenza di Tito"	
		1753 Became totally blind			
				1754-64 Director Vienna Opera	1754 "La Donna pettose"
					1755 "Alessandro nell'Indie"
1756 Composed "Auferstehung Christi"					
Greatest works were 12 separate series of cantatas and motets for the church year; in all 3000 vocal numbers with organ or orchestra accompaniment	1757 "Les Paladins"				
			1758 Opera,"Catone in Utica"		
		Died 1759 (London)			1760 "La buona figliuola"
		CHERUBINI (Maria Luigi) Born 1760 Florence, Italy	1761 "Artaserse"	1761 "Le Cadi dupé" Ballet, Don' Juan	
			1762 "Alessandro nell' Indie"	1762 "Orfeo ed Euridice"	
			1763 "Orione" "Zanaida"		
	Died 1764 (Paris)				
		1766 Began music study with his father	1765 "Adriano in Siria" Six symphonies	1765 Ballet, "Semiramide" "Telemaco"	
Died 1767 (Hamburg)			1767 "Carattaco"	1767 "Alceste"	
	BEETHOVEN (Ludwig van) Born 1770 Bonn, Germany		1770-75 Three Symphonies	1770 "Paride ed Elena"	
					1771 "Artigone"
			1772 "Temistocle"	1772 In Paris	
		1773 Wrote first Mass at thirteen years of age			
SPONTINI (Gasparo) Born 1774 Jesi, Italy				1774 Iphigénie en Aulide	

(Contd. Pl. 7, Col. 14) (Contd. Pl. 7, Col. 11) (Contd. Pl. 7, Col. 10) (Contd. Pl. 7, Col. 3) (Contd. Pl. 7, Col. 1) (Contd. Pl. 7, Co.

PLATE 6—1750—1774

7	8	9	10	11	12
HAYDN (Contd.)	GRÉTRY (Contd.)	CIMAROSA (Contd.)	SCARLATTI, D. (Contd.)	DR. ARNE (Contd.)	BOCCHERINI (Contd.)

7	8	9	10	11	12
52 Opera,"Der eue krummeTeufel"					
5 Composed first rtet					
			Died 1757 Naples		1757 Studied the 'cello and composition in Rome
58(circa) Comsed first symphony	1758 Composed six little symphonies				
			MOZART (Wolfgang Amadeus) Born 1756 Salzburg, Germany	1759 Made Doctor of Music at Oxford University	
60 Married Maria na Keller					
61 Entered serce of Count Paul terhazy at Eisenadt 1762 Prince colaus Esterhazy cceeds brother		1761-1772 Studied under Sacchini and Piccini at the Conservatoris Santa Maria di Loreto in Venice	1762 Played in Munich and Vienna	1761 Oratorio, "Judith"	
			1763 In Paris		
			1764 Met Johann Christian Bach in England		1764-9 In Municipal Orchestra at Lucca; composed two oratorios
	1765 First opera "La Vendemmiatrice"		1765 Composed his first symphony		
			1767 Composed his first oratorio		
	1768 "Le Huron"		1768 "La Finta Semplice" "Bastien and Bastienne" Conducted his own Mass		1768 In Paris as 'cellist
	1769 "Le tableau parlant"		1769-70 In Italy		1769 Settled in Madrid under patronage of the King of Spain's brother, the Infante Don Luis
0 "DerApotheker"		1770 Oratorio, "Giudetta"	1770 "Mitridate"		
	1771 "Zemire et Azor"		1771 In Salzburg and Italy "Ascanio in Alba"		
2 "Farewell" Symny		1772 First opera "Le Stravaganze del Conte" 1773 "La finta parigina"	1772 "Lucio Silla"		

ntd. Pl.7, Col.8) (Contd. Pl.7, Col.5) (Contd. Pl.7, Col.6) (Contd. Pl.7, Col.9) (Contd. Pl.7, Col.7) (Contd. Pl.7, Col.13)

Plate 7
A. D. 1775-1799

PLATE 7—1775—1799

1	2	3	4	5	
GLUCK (Contd.)	PICCINI (Contd.)	BACH, J.C. (Contd.)	SCHUBERT (Franz Peter)	GRÉTRY (Contd.)	CIMAROSA (Contd.)
1777 "Armide"	1776 "I Viaggiatori" Settled in Paris	1776 "Lucca Silla"			1777 "Il Fantast
	1778 "Roland"	1778 "La Clemenza di Scipione" 1779 "Amadis des Gaules"		1778 "L'Amant jaloux" 1779 "Aucassin et Nicolette" 1780 "Andromaque"	1779 "L'Italian in Londra"
1779 "Iphigénie en Tauride" "Echo et Narcisse"	1780 "Atys"				
		Died 1782 (London)			
	1783 "Didon"				
1785-6 Klopstock Odes				1784 "Richard Coeur de Lion" "La Caravane du Caire"	1784 "L'Olympia
Died 1787 (Vienna)					
					1788 "La Cleopa
	1789 Retired to Naples				1789-92 In Russ as chamber comp to Catherine II
MEYERBEER (Giacomo) Born 1791 Berlin, Germany				1791 "Guillaume Tell"	
					1792 "Il Matrimo Segreto
					1794 "Gli Orazi Curiozii
		DONIZETTI (Gaetano) Born 1797 Bergamo, Italy	Born 1797 Lichtenthal, near Vienna, Austria	1797 "Anacreon chez Polycrate	
1798 Piano pupil of Clementi Played in public at 7	1798 Returned to France				1799 "Semiramid

(Contd. Pl. 8, Col. 1)(Contd. Pl. 8, Col. 2)(Contd. Pl. 8, Col. 4)(Contd. Pl. 8, Col. 7)(Contd. Pl. 8, Col. 5)(Contd. Pl. 8, C

Plate 8
A. D. 1800-1824

PLATE 8-1800-1824

1	2	3	4	5	6
MEYERBEER (Contd.)	PICCINI (Contd.) Died 1800 (Paris)	PAGANINI (Contd.)	DONIZETTI (Contd.)	GRÉTRY (Contd.)	CIMAROSA (Contd.)
	BELLINI (Vincenzo) Born 1801 Catania, Sicily	1801-4 Forsook the violin for the guitar			Died 1801 (Veni
					STRAUSS (Johann, Sr. Born 1804 Vienn Austria
		1804 Locatelli's studies renew his interest. 1805-08 In court post at Lucca, Italy			
		1808 Successful concert tour of Italy	1809 Studied at Naples Conservatory		
1810-12 Studied with Abbe Vogler 1811 Oratorios "Gott und die Natur" First grand opera "Jephthas Gelübde" 1813 First comic opera "Die Beiden Kalifen"		1813 Resigned court post at Lucca		Died 1813 near Paris	1813 Ran away f home because mu study was denie him.
1815 In Venice		1816 Gave concert in Milan with Lafont, famous French violinist	1815 Entered Italian Army 1818 First opera, "Enrico di Borgogno"		
1818 "Romilda e" Constanza 1820 "Margherita d'Anjou"	1819-27 Student in Naples with Merca- dante as fellow pupil.				1919 Entered Sp er's orchestra.
		1823 Survived al- most fatal illness	1822 Opera "Zoraïde di Granata" so suc- cessful that he was granted exemption from military ser- vice		1823 In Lanner' orchestra
1824 "Il Crociato in Egitto"				SMETANA (Bedrich) Born 1824 Leitomischl, Bohemia	

(Contd. Pl.9, Col.1)(Contd. Pl.9, Col.2)(Contd. Pl.9, Col.5)(Contd. Pl.9, Col.3)(Contd.Pl.9, Col.22)(Contd.Pl.9, Col

PLATE 8—1800—1824

19 LISZT (Franz)	20 WAGNER (Richard)	21 VERDI (Giuseppe)	22 GOUNOD (Charles)	23 OFFENBACH (Jacques)	24 GLINKA (Michael)
					Born 1804 near Smolensk, Russia
1811 Raiding, ary					
	Born 1813 Leipzig, Germany Father died same year; mother married Ludwig Geyer	Born 1813 Le Roncole, near Busseto, Italy			
			Born 1818 Paris, France		1817-22 Received piano lessons from John Field during this period
				Born 1819 Cologne, Germany	
) First appear- e as a pianist at burg In Vienna	1821 Death of Ludwig Geyer	1820 First music lessons from local church organist			
			Early musical education given by his mother	Son of a cantor in the Jewish Synagogue at Cologne	
3 First public certs					1823 Composed three pieces for small orchestra

td. Pl.9, Col.15) (Contd. Pl. 9, Col. 16) (Contd. Pl.9, Col. 17) (Contd. Pl. 9, Col. 18) (Contd. Pl. 9, Col. 19) (Contd. Pl. 9, Col. 27)

Plate 9
A. D. 1825-1849

PLATE 9–1825–1849

1	2	3	4	5	6
MEYERBEER (Contd.)	BELLINI (Contd.)	DONIZETTI (Contd.)	ROSSINI (Contd.)	PAGANINI (Contd.)	SPONTINI (Contd.)
	1825 First opera, "Adelson e Salvini"		1825 Manager Theâtre Italien, Paris		1825 "Alcidor"
1826 In Paris			1826 Composer to King "Siege of Corinth"		
	1827 "Il Pirato"		1827 "Moise" (Paris revision)		
			1828 "Le Compte Ory"	1828-31 In Vienna, Berlin, Paris, London	
	1829 "La Straniero"		1829 "William Tell"		1829 Last compl opera, "Agnes v Hohenstaufen"
	1830 "I Capuletti e Montecchi"	1830 "Anna Bolena"			1830-41 Worked opera based on M ton's "Paradise Lost"
1831 "Robert le Diable"	1831 "Sonnambula" "Norma"				
		1832 "Elisir d'Amore"	1832-41 "Stabat Mater"		
	1833 "Beatrice di Tenda"	1833 "Lucrezia Borgia"			
	1834 "I Puritani" Died near Paris				
		1835 "Lucia di Lammermoor" "Marino Faliero"	1836-47 At Bologna		
1836 "Les-Huguenots"					
	BIZET (Georges) Born 1838 Paris, France				
		1840 "La Fille du Regiment" "La Favorita"		Died 1840 Nice	1840 Quarrel wi Court Opera Officials
		1841 "Maria Padilla"		SULLIVAN (Arthur S.) Born 1841 London, England	
1842-43 Composed "Le Prophête"		1842 "Linda da Chamounix"			1842 Convicted lèse-majesté Retired to Ital
		1843 "Maria di Rohan" "Don Pasquale"			
1844 "Das Feldlager in Schlesien"		1844 "Don Sebastiano"			1844 Conducted "La Vestale" in Dresden at Wagn invitation
			1845 Death of first wife		
			1847 Married Olympe Pelissier		
	1848 Entered Conservatory at ten	Died 1848 (Bergamo)			
1849 "Le Prophete" produced					

(Contd. Pl. 10, Col. 1) (Contd. Pl. 10, Col. 2)   (Contd. Pl. 10, Col. 3) (Contd. Pl. 10, Col. 26) (Contd. Pl. 10, Co

Plate 10
A. D. 1850-1874

PLATE 10—1850—1874

1	2	3	4	5	6
MEYERBEER (Contd.)	BIZET (Contd.)	ROSSINI (Contd.)	SPONTINI (Contd.)	BERLIOZ (Contd.)	BRAHMS (Contd.)

			Died 1851 (Near Jesi)		1851 Scherzo i E flat Minor
				1852 In London	
					1853 Piano Son in C and F sha Minor
1854 "L'Étoile du Nord"				1854 First wife died Marriage to Marie Recio	Tour with Reme Met Joachim, Li and the Schuma 1854-58 In Detm Composed Piano certo No.1 in D nor and 4 ball
		1855 Returned to Paris			
	1857 Prix de Rome "Le Docteur Miracle"				
	1858 "Don Procopia"		PUCCINI (Giacomo) Born 1858 Lucca, Italy	1858-63 "Les Troyens"	1858 Serenade
1859 "Dinorah"	1859 "La Guzla de l'Emir"				1859 Played fi piano concerto Leipzig 1860 Serenade (Revised 1875) 1861 Piano Con in D Minor Piano Quartet G Minor
				1862 "Béatrice et Bénedict" Death of second wife 1863 "Les Troyens" produced	Piano Quartet 1862 Went to Vi Sextet in B fl Handel Variati
	1863 "Pearl Fishers"				
Died 1864 (Paris)		1864 Petite Messe Solonelle			1863-64 Conduc Vienna Singaka Piano Quintet Paganini Varia
1865 "L'Africaine" produced (Paris) Begun 1838					1866 Sextet in 'Cello Sonata E Minor
	1867 "La Jolie Fille de Perth"			1867 Death of son	
		Died 1868 (Passy)			1868 German Req
				Died 1869 (Paris)	1869 Liebeslie Waltzes Cantata "Rinal
	1871 "Numa"			VAUGHAN WILLIAMS (Ralph) Born 1872 Down Ampney, near Cirencester, England	1871 Schicksal
	1872 "Djamileh" "L'Arlésienne" music	RACHMANINOFF (Serge) Born 1873 Onega, Russia			1872 Triumphli
SCHÖNBERG (Arnold) Born 1874 Vienna, Austria					1873 Quartet i C Minor Variations on T by Haydn

(Contd. Pl. 11, Col. 35)(Contd. Pl. 11, Col. 16)(Contd. Pl. 11, Col. 32)(Contd. Pl. 11, Col. 11)(Contd. Pl. 11, Col. 20)(Contd. Pl. 11,

PLATE 10—1850—1874

31	32	33	34	35	36
BORODIN (Contd.)	MOUSSORGSKY (Contd.)	TSCHAIKOWSKY (Contd.)	RIMSKY-KORSAKOW (Contd.)	JANÁČEK (Leoš)	LOEFFLER (Martin)
				Born 1854 Hukvaldy, Moravia	
		1855—58 Piano studies with Kundinger			
			1856 Educated for Naval career		
—62 In Government post	1857 Comes under influence of Mily Balakireff				
		1859 Graduated from law school			
		1861 Studied with Zaremba	1861 Met Balakireff and his group		Born 1861 Mülhausen, Alsace (France)
			1862—65 At sea as Naval cadet Visited America		
	1863 In clerical post, St. Petersburg "Salaambo"	1863 In Conservatory at St. Petersburg 1864 "Romeo and Juliet" Overture			
			1865 Symphony	1865 Chorister at Brno Studied with Krizkovsky	
		1866—74 Taught at Moscow Conservatory "Voyevode"			
Symphony in at	1867 "Sennacherib"	"Undine"	1867 Tone-poem, "Sadko" (revised 1891)		
	1868 "The Marriage"				
	1870 "The Nursery"				
			1871 Professor of composition at Conservatory in St. Petersburg 1873 Detached from Navy		
		1872—76 Music critic			
	1874 "Boris Godounoff (Several revisions) "Pictures at an Exhibition"	1874 "The Guardsman"	"The Maid of Pskov"		

td. Pl. 11, Col. 30) (Contd. Pl. 11, Col. 28) (Contd. Pl. 11, Col. 29) (Contd. Pl. 11, Col. 31) (Contd. Pl. 11, Col. 27) (Contd. Pl. 11, Col. 37)

Plate 11
A. D. 1875-1899

PLATE II—1875—1899

1	2	3	4	5	6
BRAHMS (Contd.)	RUBINSTEIN (Contd.)	LISZT (Contd.)	WAGNER (Contd.)	VERDI (Contd.)	GOUNOD (Contd.)
	1875 opera, "The Demon"	1875 Head of Hungarian Academy			1875 Returned Paris
1876 Quartet in B flat		1876 Deaths of Countess d'Agoult and George Sand	1876 First Ring cycle (Bayreuth) 1876-82 Composed "Parsifal" 1877 Conductor in London		
1877 Symphony No. 1 in C Minor					1877 "Cinq Mars"
1878 Symphony No. 2 in D					1878 "Polyeucte"
1879 Violin Concerto	1879 Opera, "Nero"				
1880 Two Rhapsodies Violin Sonata in G		1880-85 Peak of fame as teacher			
1881 "Academic Festival" Overture				1881 Revised version of "Simon Boccanegra" (Milan)	
1882 Piano Concerto No. 2 in B flat			1882 "Parsifal" at Bayreuth Died 1883 (Venice)		1882 "The Redemp[tion]" Messe Solonelle
1883 "Gesang der Parzen" (Chorus)					
1884 Symphony No. 3 in F					
	1885-87 Tours		BERG (Alban) Born 1885 Vienna, Austria		1885 "Mors et V[ita]"
1886 Symphony No. 4 in E Minor		Died 1886 (Bayreuth)			
1887 Violin Sonata in A 'Cello Sonata in F				1887 "Otello"	
1888 Double Concerto for violin and 'cello					
1889 Violin sonata in D					
	1890 Resided in Berlin				
		PROKOFIEFF (Serge) Born 1891 Ekaterinoslav, Russia			
1892 Clarinet quintet Seven Fantasies and three Intermezzi for piano	1892 In Dresden				
				1893 "Falstaff"	Died 1893 (Paris)
	Died 1894 (St. Petersburg)				
Died 1897 (Vienna)				1897 Death of second wife 1898 Four Sacred Pieces	

(Contd. Pl. 12, Col. 31) (Contd. Pl. 12, Col. 24) (Contd. Pl. 12, Col. 3)

Plate 12
A. D. 1900-1924

PLATE 12—1900—1924

	1	2	3	4	5	6
	SULLIVAN (Contd.) Died 1900 (London)	SAINT-SAËNS (Contd.)	VERDI (Contd.)	DVOŘÁK (Contd.) 1900 "Russalka"	WOLF (Contd.)	FALLA (Contd.)
		1901 "Les Barbares"	Died 1901 (Milan)	1901 Director of Prague Conservatory		
		1902 "Parysatis"				
				1903 "Armida" Died 1904 (Prague)	Died 1903 (Vienna)	
		1905 "Hélène"				1905 Won opera with "La vida br
		1906 In America				
		1907 Attended un- veiling of own statue in Paris				1907-14 In Par Met Ravel, Debu and Dukas
		1913 Oratorio "The Promised Land"				1914 Took up re dence in Granac
		1915 In America				1915 Ballet "E amor bruja" 1916 "Nights in Gardens of Spain piano and orches
						1919 "Three-cor Hat" (final for
		Died 1921 (Algiers)				
						1923 Puppet ope "El Retablo de Maese Pedro"

(Contd. Pl. 13, Co

Plate 13
A. D. 1925-1936

PLATE 13 — 1925 — 1936

1	2	3	4	5	6
STRAUSS, R. (Contd.)	SIBELIUS (Contd.)	SCHÖNBERG (Contd.)	VAUGHAN-WILLIAMS (Contd.)	ELGAR (Contd.)	DELIUS (Contd.)
	1925 Symphony No. 7		1925 "Flos campi" Suite for viola solo Concerto Accademico (violin and orchestra) 1926 Oratorio "Sancta Civitas"		
	1926 Music for "The Tempest" "Tapiola" 1927 Piano Pieces Op. 101 and 103	1927 Quartet No. 3, Op. 30			
1928 "The Egyptian Helen"	1928 "Danse Champêtre" Op.106 for violin and piano	1928 Variations for Orchestra			
	1930 Violin Pieces Op. 115 and Op. 116				
1933 "Arabella"		1933-35 In America			
				Died 1934 (Marl Bank Worcester, England)	Died 1934 (Gre sur-Loring, Fra
1935 "Shweigsame Frau"		1935 Concerto for Violoncello and Orchestra (after the concerto for clavicembalo by Georg Matthias Monn) Suite for String Orchestra 1936 Chamber Symphony Concerto for string quartet and orchestra – (after the concerto grosso Op.6 No.7 by G.F. Handel)	1935 Symphony in F Minor French and English Folk Songs Choral Work "Five Tudor Portraits" 1936 Choral Work "Dona Nobis Pacem" Concerto for Pianoforte and Orchestra Operetta "The Poisoned Kiss" Suite for Viola and Orchestra The Running Set (2 pianos)		
1936 Olympic Hymn					

PLATE 13—1925—1936

19	20
IASKOVSKY (Contd.) Symphony No.8 Sonata No.4	FALLA (Contd.) 1925 Suite Es- pagnole for orchestra
Symphony No.9	·
Symphony No. 10 Sonata No.4	1928 Concerto for Harpsichord with flute, oboe, clarinet, violin and 'cello.
Symphony No. 11	
Symphony No.12 Symphonic hes ilbte Blatter" n Bagatelles iano) Second String et Symphony No.13	
Symphony No. 14	
Symphony No.15	
IASKOVSKY (Contd.)	FALLA (Contd.)